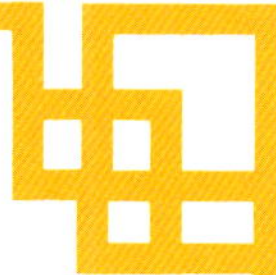

CHINESE NEW YEAR FOR KIDS

PARTY IDEAS
DRAGON PARADES
LION DANCES
ART PROJECTS
ZODIAC GAMES

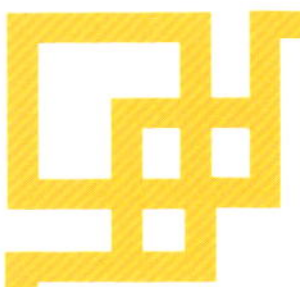

This book is dedicated to my favorite playmates,
my children,
Kevin, Tommy, Ben, Tanner, Sam & Dani

ISBN 0-9707332-5-9

Published in 2002 by

www.chinasprout.com

China Sprout, Inc. 110 W 32th St.

New York, NY 10001

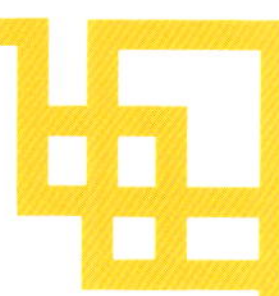

Contents

年
福

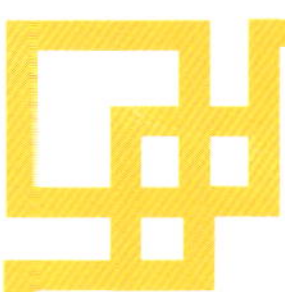

Chinese New Year Explained

Many countries celebrate the first day of the New Year in the same way. In America, we have a big party and count down the seconds to the New Year. At the stroke of midnight, which brings in the New Year, Americans celebrate with lots of yelling, screaming, horns, balloons, fireworks and kissing the ones you love. In China, the arrival of the New Year is celebrated much the same way, with family and lots of noise!

There are many differences though, between the American New Year and the Chinese New Year. First, the eastern and western calendars are not the same. In America, the calendar is based on a solar (sun) year, which is the number of days it takes the earth to go around the sun. China's calendar is based on the lunar (moon) year. America's first day of the New Year is always January 1st. In China, the first day of the New Year lands on a different day every year, according to the moon's rotation around the earth. In 2000, the Chinese New Year started on February 5th. In 2001, it was January 24.

In China, each New Year is named after one of 12 animals. The legend is that the Jade Emperor of Heaven invited all the animals of the land to a race. He told them that the first twelve animals to win the race would have a year named after them. The very tricky, yet smart Rat won the race. So Rat is the first year in the cycle. The other winners in order are Ox, Tiger, Rabbit, Dragon, Snake, Horse, Goat, Monkey, Rooster, Dog, and Pig. Every 12 years, the zodiac starts over again with Rat First.

In China, the New Year starts by thoroughly cleaning the house. This is to 'sweep out' the bad luck, and to insure good luck in the New Year. The house is then decorated with fresh flowers to represent a 'new beginning' in

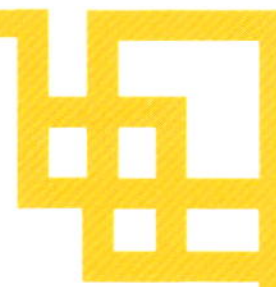
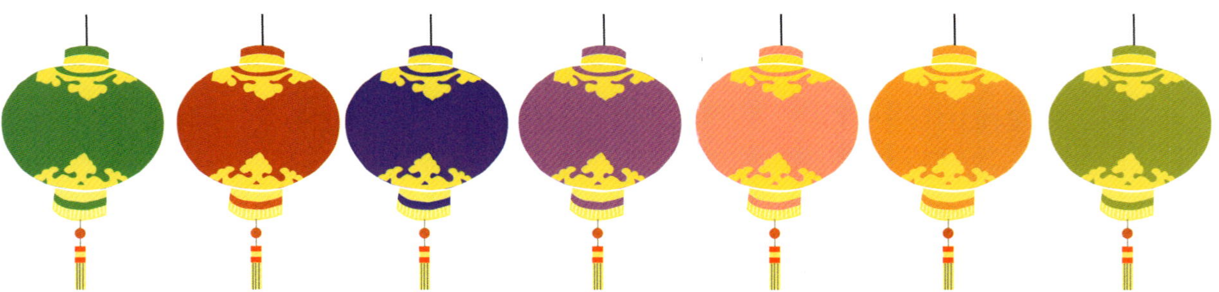

the New Year. Red scrolls are written and hung on both sides of the front door. The scrolls have wise words on them, wishing for good luck and happiness. Another way to insure good luck is to wear your best or new clothes on New Year's Day.

In China, a traditional outfit is called a 'cheongsam' (chun-sam). At midnight, the family prays to their ancestors for a good year, then they light thousands of firecrackers! The firecrackers are used to scare away evil spirits. The whole family then sits down to a very fancy dinner.

For children in China, the best part of the New Year celebration comes at the stroke of midnight: Everyone in the country turns a year older at the same moment! Children in China receive a small gift on New Year's Day. Red envelopes with 'Good Luck Money' in them are given to children by their parents and relatives. It is also common for adults to exchange fruits, cakes, and flowers with friends and relatives.

The next day, people go to visit more family and friends. From small villages to big cities, there are huge Chinese New Year parades, with Lion Dancers, fireworks and a very long Dragon at the end of the parade. So, congratulations! Today is your birthday in China. You are another year older!

Chinese New Year Calendar

Chinese Year	Zodiac Animal	Western Year
4698	Dragon	February 5, 2000
4699	Snake	January 24, 2001
4700	Horse	February 12, 2002
4701	Sheep	February 1, 2003
4702	Monkey	January 22, 2004
4703	Rooster	February 9, 2005
4704	Dog	January 29, 2006
4705	Pig	February 18, 2007
4706	Rat	February 7, 2008
4707	Ox	January 26, 2009
4708	Tiger	February 10, 2010
4709	Rabbit	February 3, 2011
4710	Dragon	January 23, 2012
4711	Snake	February 10, 2013
4712	Horse	January 31, 2014
4713	Sheep	February 19, 2015
4714	Monkey	February 9, 2016
4715	Rooster	January 28, 2017
4716	Dog	February 16, 2018
4717	Pig	February 5, 2019

晚
会

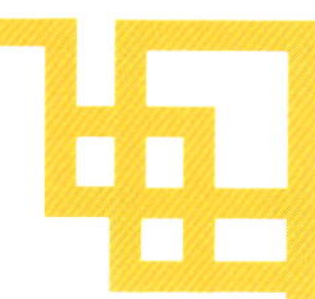

Chinese New Year Parties at School

The following is a list of ideas to help introduce the Chinese New Year in the classroom. All projects and ideas are inexpensive to make for a large group and materials are easily found at the grocery or craft store.

1. Introduction: Get the kids settled on the rug for story time. Sit in a chair in front of them. Then have them stand up and copy what you do. Put your hands together like you're praying, with your hands about chest level. Next slightly bow your head and say Ni Hao. Have the children bow back to you and say Ni Hao to you. You have just said hello in Chinese!

2. Name Tags: Have the kids sit down. Next, have them choose a Chinese name. Put the names on name tags for the kids to wear during the party.

Boy's Names: Da Wei, Ke Ming, Hong Shan
Girl's Names: Mei-Mei, Ling, Ping

3. World Map: Get out a world map or a globe and show the kids the location of China. Show them where the United States is in relation to China. Talk about how someone might get to China from the United States.

4. World Ball: Have preschoolers roll a world ball to each other, letting each child find China on the globe. (Mark China with a sticker.) Then each child wins a Good Luck Red Envelope with gold foil chocolate coins or stickers inside. (See page 28)

5. Read Out Loud the introduction "The Chinese New Year Explained" to the children.

6. Zodiac Games: (See page 24) For kids 3-12 years old. Led by an adult.

7. Lion Dance: (Page 16) This gets the whole class involved! It can be performed indoors or outdoors. For ages 3-12.

8. Dragon Parade: (Pages 20) The kids can make the dragon in the classroom as an art project or an adult can make the dragon beforehand. The parade can go through the school hallways, visiting other classrooms or held outside during recess or P.E. (A basketball court is the perfect place.) Have the kids go around in a big circle, making sure all children get a turn to be under the dragon.

9. Dragon Eye Opening Ceremony: (Page 22) For good luck, new dragons go through this ceremony.

10. Kids' Art: Kids will enjoy the Dragon puppet art project on page 29, Lantern worksheet on page 23, or making their own 'Good Luck Red Envelopes' on page 28.

11. Snacks: (See page 27)

12. Good Luck Red Envelopes: At the end of the party, ask the teacher to hand out the good luck red envelopes. The children have to show respect to their elders before receiving the envelopes. Fill the envelopes with either chocolate gold foil coins, stickers, or crisp one dollar bills before hand. Have the children get in line and one by one have them bow to their teacher. (To do this put your hands together at the chest, like praying, then add a slight bow of the head.) Before the teacher hands out the red envelope, the child is to say "Thank you for being my teacher."

Chinese New Year Parties at Home

Invite all of your child's friends! (They don't have to be Asian, all kids enjoy sharing this cultural experience.) This is a theme party, so start out with fun invitations. Invitations could arrive in Good Luck Red Envelopes. (See pages 28) On the invitation, ask each guest to dress either in red for good luck or wear a Chinese outfit.

At the kitchen or dinning room table, have the lantern worksheet with washable markers. In the TV room, play travel videos from China with the sound off. Play Chinese music throughout the whole party. About halfway through the party, clear off the coloring table and serve dinner... Chinese food of course! When it gets dark, have a dragon parade in the backyard or on the sidewalks in your neighborhood. (See page 20) As the kids leave, hand out Good Luck Red Envelopes as party favors. (See page 28)

Party decorations could be colorful strings of Christmas lights in the coloring room and two identical long red banners hanging on each side of the front door. The banners have wishes of good luck and good health on them. These banners can be made from three pieces of red 8 ½" X 11" paper taped together length-

wise. Hang paper lanterns either inside the house or outside by the front door. Paper lanterns can be purchased at party supply stores.

Ambitious parents could do the Dragon Puppet on page 29 with older kids during the party or teach the kids to do a lion dance (see page 16.)

Ancestor Worship During the Chinese New Year

Ancestors

Ancestor Worship is the spiritual basis of Chinese culture. It is often the single most important religious aspect in Chinese homes. In China, your ancestors protect your family from evil spirits, disease, misfortune and plain old bad luck. At the stroke of midnight on the eve of Chinese New Year, Chinese families gather around the ancestors' altar in their homes. They say thank you for all their help and ask for guidance in the coming year. Ancestors are very much like Western culture's concept of 'guardian angels'.

To pray to an ancestor, you bang a gong several times. (This is like ringing a door bell to the ancestors. It's how you call them into your home.) Next get down on your hands and knees to show respect, and then bow up and down three times while holding burning incense. Then say a prayer asking your ancestors to watch over you.

To honor your ancestors, put photos of your deceased relatives on a table. A red candle goes on either side of the photos. The candles represent the sun and the moon. These are very important figures in Chinese culture. Next, a tiny pot of sand goes in front of the ancestral photo. Incense is lit and a prayer is said. The incense sticks are put in the pot of sand and allowed to burn down. Incense represents the stars. The smell of incense is to please the ancestors. Offerings of food also go on this table. These should be the ancestors' favorite foods, plus oranges for good luck. A bowl of rice with the chopsticks standing up would also go on the altar.

Buddhist 'prayer money' is burned for the ancestors. When the smoke moves, it is said the ancestors are accepting the offering. (It is best to do this outside!)

On the first day of the Chinese New Year, the whole family sits down to an elaborate dinner. To show respect, they set an empty plate out to 'invite the ancestors to dinner.'

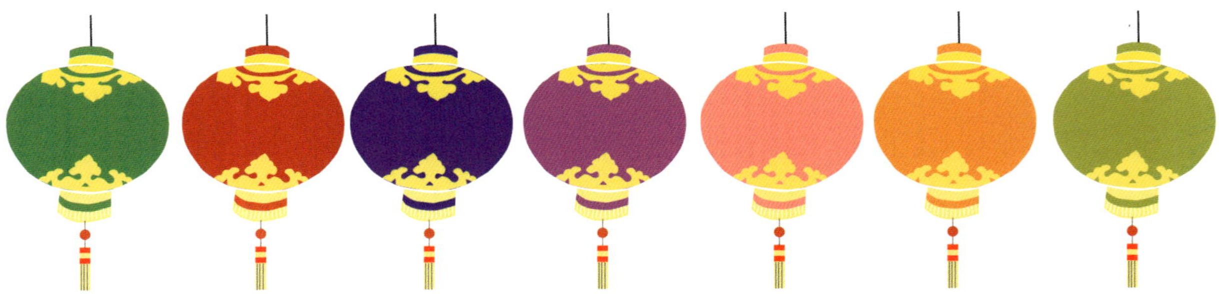

Buddhist Prayer Money

This 'fake money' is used as an offering to your ancestors. You burn it, and when the wind moves the smoke, it is said the ancestors are receiving your offering.

Note the wording on the bill. It says 'Hell Bank'. That is to trick the evil spirits into thinking this is not good money. Buddhist Prayer Money, along with incense sticks, can be purchased at any large Chinese grocery store.

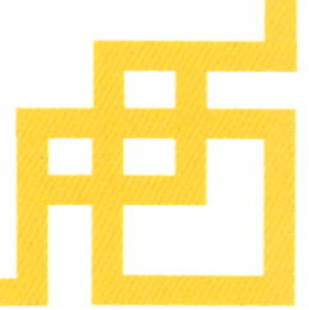

Lion Dance Activity

It is an honor to be chosen to do a lion dance. Karate students usually perform this dance. The lion dance comes from China and is performed on the Chinese New Year and other special occasions like a wedding or the Moon Festival. The lion dance is used to scare away evil spirits and bring good luck. Lion dancers perform in front of stores on New Year's Day to ensure good luck all year to the store owners.

This dance came from China around 400 BC. The Hans attacked village farmers riding on the backs of elephants, and destroyed everything they owned. The farmers had no way to protect themselves and were defenseless, so they made colorful costumes like lions. When the Hans would come on the backs of elephants, the farmers would jump out in their lion costumes and dance. The colorful lions jumping around would scare the elephants and the elephants would run away, ruining the Hans attack plan.

To perform a lion dance, use two colorful bed sheets or table cloths. This will make two lions. Choose 4 children to dance. One Child is the head of the lion and the other the tail. Have these 4 students pretend fight like lions, but never actually touch each other. The lion dancers should stretch like a lion, bend down, and challenge the other lion. The submissive lion should lie down on the floor and roll over like a dog would to have its belly rubbed. To make the lion look like it's standing up on its hind legs, have the biggest kid in the class put the smallest kid in the class on their shoulders, all while under the sheet. Have the other students rhythmically beat a gong, cymbals, rhythm instruments, cooking pots, drums, or tambourines the entire time the kids are performing the lion dance. Let groups of four try the dance for one minute at a time. You will also need one child to be the Buddha. Rotate students until all kids in the class have had a turn.

The Buddha in a lion dance acts like a clown/lion tamer in a circus. (See page 18 for mask) He is the comic relief. The Buddha teases the lion with a long string with lettuce tied to the end. The lion gets mad and chases the Buddha. The lion tries to catch the lettuce to eat it. The Buddha keeps the lettuce away from the lion until the end of the dance. Then the lion pretends to eat the lettuce. In a real lion dance, money is hidden in the lettuce. All proceeds from the lion dance would go to a local charity. This is a very lively, noisy event and the kids love it! Have fun!

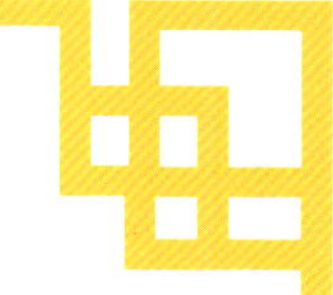

Dragon Parade

The purpose of the dragon parade is to scare away evil spirits to ensure good luck for the New Year. The dragon is very special. He breathes clouds and flies above China to protect it from evil spirits. The dragon is only brought out once a year during the Chinese New Year parade. The dragon is said to chase the sun around and around the world. This is why we have night and day.

This dragon can hold about fifteen kids under it. It is great for class parties or a Chinese New Year Party at home. One kid leads the parade banging a gong or trash can lid wearing a Buddha mask. (See page 18.) The Buddha carries the 'Sun', and the Dragon chases them.

Put 10-15 kids under the dragon. Then have the rest of the kids following behind the dragon beating rhythm instruments or blowing party horns. You could have the parade in the halls of school, around the basketball court, during recess, or at home in your backyard or on the sidewalks.

Materials:

1 large box for the head
1 shoe box for the mouth
Clear packing tape
Stapler
Two cheap red plastic table cloths
Yellow or red plastic cups

Card board
Pillow stuffing or cotton
White card stock paper
Red and yellow wrapping paper
Patterned wrapping paper
2 paper towel tubes

Directions:

1. Cover the outside of both boxes in solid red or yellow wrapping paper. (It is easiest to wrap it like a gift using clear packing tape for strength.)

2. Add a strip of colorful wrapping paper down the middle of the face.

3. The ears, eyes and nose are made from either red or yellow plastic cups. Draw black circles on the end of the cup to make the eyes. Attach with clear packing tape.

4. The mustache, beard and eyebrows are made from pillow stuffing glued to white card stock paper.

5. The horns are paper towel tubes covered in wrapping paper. Attach with clear packing tape.

6. The dinosaur-like spikes on the top of the head are cut from card board and covered in wrapping paper. Tabs are cut for stability. Attach with clear packing tape.

7. For the tail, take two long, cheap, red plastic tablecloths and connect them end-to-end lengthwise. First tape the seams together and then staple over the tape.

8. Next, wrap one end of the tablecloth around a strip of cardboard. Attach that end to the back of the dragon's head using clear packing tape and staples. It will be very sturdy.

9. To make the 'Sun' that the Buddha carries, color a paper plate yellow on both sides. Attach the plate to the end of a yard stick with tape.

10. Now go have a parade!

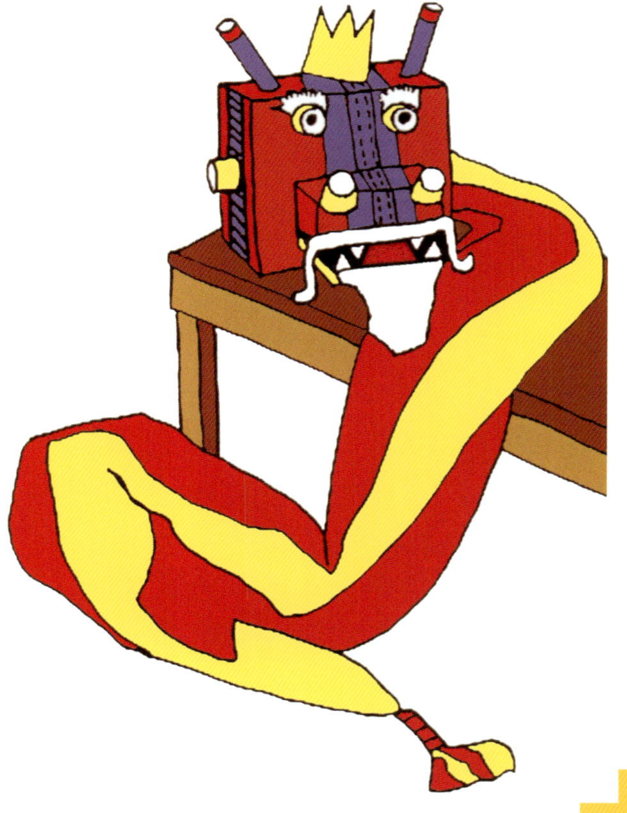

The Dragon Eye Opening Ceremony

Before a new dragon is used in a parade, there is a dragon eye opening ceremony for good luck. To start, bang on a gong 3 times to wake the dragon up. (Pots and pans can also be used). Then pretend to light red candles and incense sticks. Next use a red marker and draw on the dragon's eyes. Now your dragon is awake and ready for the parade!

Write a riddle about a zodiac animal in this box. Hide your answer somewhere on the lantern. Color the lantern. Have your friends guess the riddle.

Zodiac Games

"Who Am I?" game. Show the kids the zodiac animals, then read the clues to the kids and have them guess the animal you are talking about. They are very easy, but educational. Kindergartens through 5th graders enjoy this game.

Clues:

1. I am a make believe animal. Who am I? (Dragon)
2. My name rhymes with fox.(Ox)
3. I say oink. (Pig)
4. My name rhymes with log. (Hog)
5. I swing from my tail. (Monkey)
6. My name rhymes with wagon. (Dragon)
7. I fly and chase the sun. (Dragon)
8. I look like Puma. (Pig)
9. I love to hop. (Rabbit)
10. My name rhymes with chunky. (Monkey)
11. This is the Year of the __?
12. People ride on my back. I plow fields. (Ox)
13. My name rhymes with jeep. (Sheep)
14. My name rhymes with mat. (Rat)
15. I have a mane. (Horse)
16. I am a long thin reptile. (Snake)
17. My name rhymes with rake. (Snake)
18. I am only seen once a year in a Chinese New Year parade. (Dragon)
19. My name rhymes with cat. (Rat)
20. I fly over China and protect it from evil spirits. If you see me flying during the Chinese New Year, you will have good luck all year! (Dragon)
21. I bark and I am a good pet. (Dog)
22. I am a large cat with stripes. (Tiger)
23. I am a large strong bull. (Ox)
24. I am a male chicken. (Rooster)

Additional Game: Make two photocopies of the zodiac animals. Laminate the sheets. Cut into individual squares and play a memory matching game.

RAT

OX

TIGER

RABBIT

DRAGON

SNAKE

HORSE

GOAT

MONKEY

ROOSTER

DOG

PIG

Classroom Snacks to Celebrate The Chinese New Year at School

1. Serve Asian Rice in red plastic bowls with chopsticks. Rice and chopsticks can be purchased in the Chinese food section of the grocery store. In China, it is acceptable to pick up the bowl and scrape the rice into your mouth using chopsticks. A large belch at the end of a meal is a compliment to the cook. May serve with soy sauce or butter. <u>No forks allowed!</u> Only give the children chopsticks to eat with. Show them how to use them and let them figure it out. They'll have a blast!

2. Chinese Dumplings and Egg Rolls. One per person. Dumplings can be purchased in the Chinese food section of the grocery store and egg rolls can be purchased in the frozen section of the grocery store. Serve with sweet and sour sauce.

3. Chinese Fortune Cookies and Chinese Almond Cookies. These can be purchased in the Chinese section of the grocery store. They come individually wrapped and in a box. The kids are thoroughly entertained with the fortune cookies!

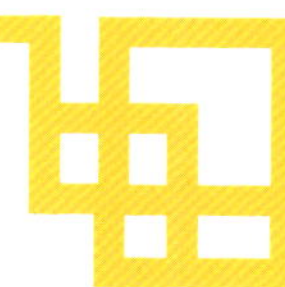

Good Luck Red Money Envelopes

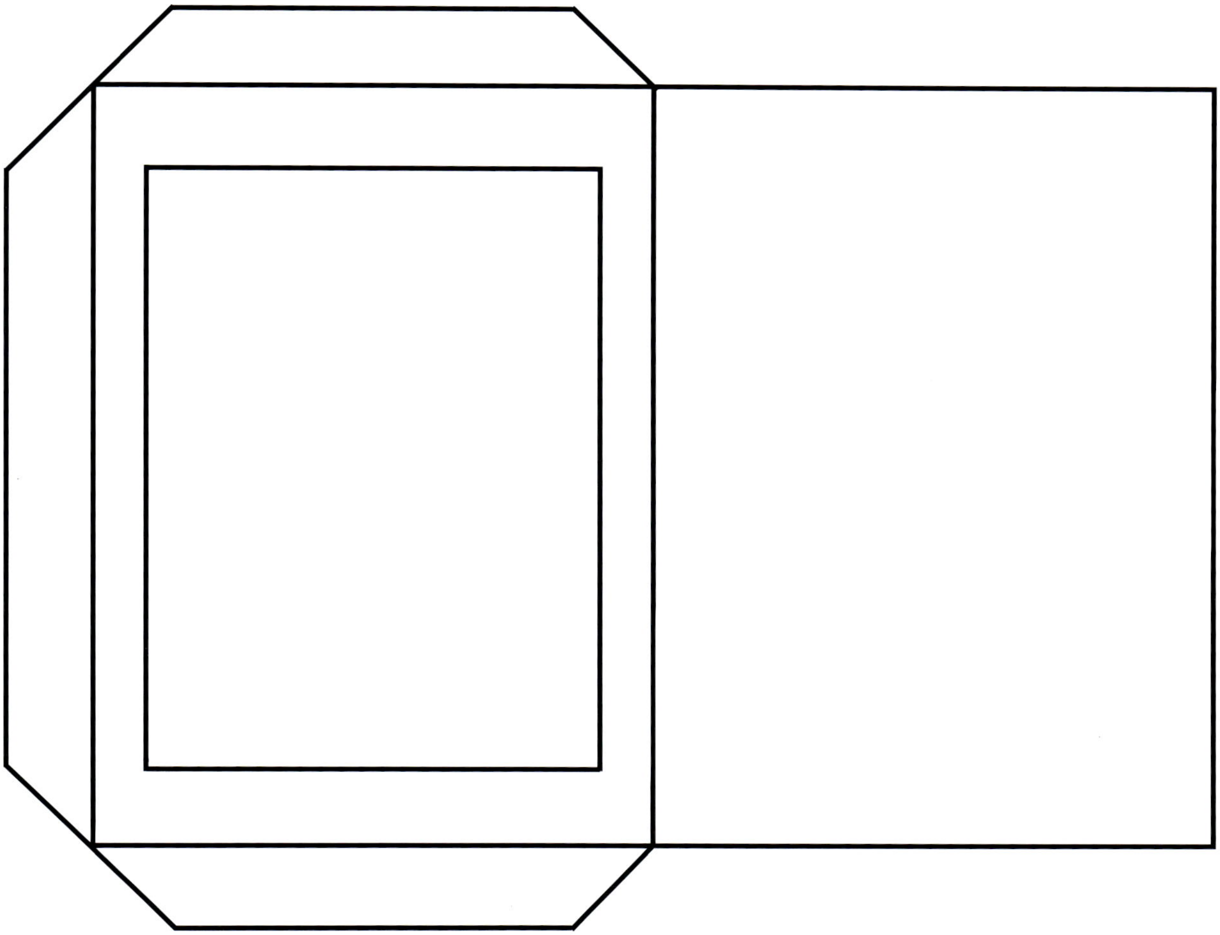

In celebration of the Chinese New Year, children and unmarried people are given red envelopes with a brand new dollar bill in them. They are given these red envelopes by relatives and close friends of the family.

You can put gold foil chocolate coins, stickers, or a fresh crisp one-dollar bill in each envelope. Photocopy the black and white version onto red paper and have the children decorate the envelopes with zodiac animals. Fold at the seams and glue shut. Then exchange with friends, or have the teacher pass them out.

Dragon Puppet

All materials come from a craft store or the grocery store. This is an inexpensive project for large groups of kids. These directions are for one Puppet.

Materials:

1 red plastic cup, 16 oz.
3 one inch pom-poms, any color
Two 1/4 -inch plastic jiggly eyes
2 silver disk sequins
Yellow Felt
Red Felt
1 pipe cleaner, any color
24" x 5" strip of wrapping paper
2 small gold bells
"Tacky craft glue"

Directions:

1. Glue two pom-poms to the top of the cup for the eyes. Glue two jiggly eyes to the pom-poms.

2. At the other end of the cup, add one more pom-pom for the nose. Glue two silver sequins to the nose for the nostrils.

3. For the horns, cut and glue two yellow triangles on both sides of the nose, 1 ½" X 3" each. The horns should hang off the end of the cup.

4. Punch two holes on the bottom of the cup. Thread one pipe cleaner through both holes so the

pipe cleaner is on the outside. Twist the pipe cleaners around a pencil to make them wacky!

5. Cut and glue a 2" X 6" red triangle tongue to the inside of the cup. Have the tongue hang outside the cup.

6. Cut, then glue two 2" X 3" red triangles for the ears. Place them on the bottom of the cup. Push the antenna horns up and glue the ears over them. The ears should be sticking out on both sides behind the eyes.

7. Measure and cut the colorful wrapping paper. Fold it in half lengthwise and glue the seam shut. Fold the tail accordion style about every three inches. Glue to the back of the head, over the ears.

8.When the puppet dries, hold his head under his chin, when you walk his tail will fly like a kite.

***Note:** Tacky glue is very important. School glue will not work on plastic cups.